D1809560

Positions I:

WHERE DO WE GO?

Written by Lindsay & Seth Little

Illustrated by Mark Harmon

LearnSport Books PUBLISHING CO

Meyer & Meyer Sport

British Library Cataloguing in Publication Data

A catalogue record for this book is available from the British Library

Where do we go?

All rights reserved, especially the right to copy and distribute, including the translation rights. No part of this work may be reproduced—including by photocopy, microfilm or any other means—processed, stored electronically, copied or distributed in any form whatsoever without the written permission of the publisher.

© 1st Ed. 2016 by LearnSport Books. All rights reserved.
© 2nd Ed. 2016 by LearnSport Books and Meyer & Meyer Sport

Aachen, Auckland, Beirut, Cairo, Cape Town, Dubai, Hägendorf, Hong Kong, Indianapolis, Manila, New Delhi, Singapore, Sydney, Tehran, Vienna

Member of the World Sport Publishers' Association (WSPA)

Manufacturing: Print Consult GmbH, Munich, Germany

ISBN 978-1-78255-098-3
E-Mail: info@m-m-sports.com, service@learnsportbooks.com
www.m-m-sports.com
www.learnsportbooks.com

May 2016

My Life in Soccer

by Yael Averbuch

Soft, green grass. Fun times with my family. Love and joy. Those are some of the first things that come to mind when I think about soccer.

I was seven years old when I watched my first soccer game. I didn't know anything about the sport besides that it seemed fun. My best friend in school invited me to come watch her game and my dad took me to cheer for her. That day, her team needed extra players and they asked me if I would play. I was very shy and said no. After watching her game, though, I decided that it looked like a lot of fun so my dad signed me up to play on a recreational team the next season.

I fell in love with the game at my first soccer practice, and have loved it ever since. It was a special time to share with my dad, as we learned about the game together. It was fun to be out on the field with my teammates and getting to play. And it was a whole new set of skills and experiences that made me very excited to learn.

When I was nine I wrote in my journal that I wanted to be a professional soccer player. I didn't really understand at the time what that meant, and

I certainly didn't know what it would take to get there. But I knew that I wanted to play for as long as I could and be the best I could be.

Since that time, soccer has taken me all across the world. I have played all over the U.S., in England, Germany, Holland, Japan, China, Australia, New Zealand, Thailand, Mexico, Canada, Sweden, Russia, Serbia and many other countries! I have also played for my country. I have formed friendships playing soccer that will last a lifetime. I have also learned a lot about myself through the game. I have learned what it takes to be a champion, and also how to overcome disappointments along the way.

Soccer is called "the beautiful game." There are so many reasons the sport is so beautiful and I'm sure that you will understand them as you play. I love soccer because there is such a variety of skills to learn. There are physical skills (like running fast, being strong, playing aggressively), skills with the ball (dribbling, trapping, shooting), and skills like teamwork and leadership. All are important to the game. There is no one right way to play soccer. It is a game of imagination and creativity.

I am now living the dream I have had since I was nine years old. I am a professional soccer player. It has not always been an easy path to accomplish my goals, but whenever I practice or play, I continue to love soccer more than ever.

Soon after I started playing, my dad and I began a mission to learn the game together. We would watch videos of soccer training and try to do the same drills in my backyard. I hope that you will enjoy learning and practicing the same way I did then, and have continued to do all my career.

I encourage you to learn and play the game of soccer, but most importantly, have fun while you do!

Learn more about Yael Averbuch on her website: www.yaelaverbuch.com
Yael is also the founder of the Techne Futbol Training System, which helps players develop the skills necessary to play soccer and have fun: www.technefutbol.com

Hi! I'm Alex. Let me tell you about my team's best practice this year. It was really exciting but a little scary. It was the practice just before our first game against our rivals, the Dynamo.

As we got ready to practice, Sam started laughing. "My feet are already soaked!" she said. I smile back at her. I love everything about soccer, including the wet field.

This is my little sister, Bailee...

Coach started practice by putting us into **positions**. "We're going to play a 3-2-1 formation this week. Alex! You will be playing forward."

Forwards are responsible for creating scoring opportunities and taking shots on goal. They are also the first line of defense.

I ran across the grass to my position and got ready. My cleats soaked up water as I ran. I could hear other players squishing on the wet field too.

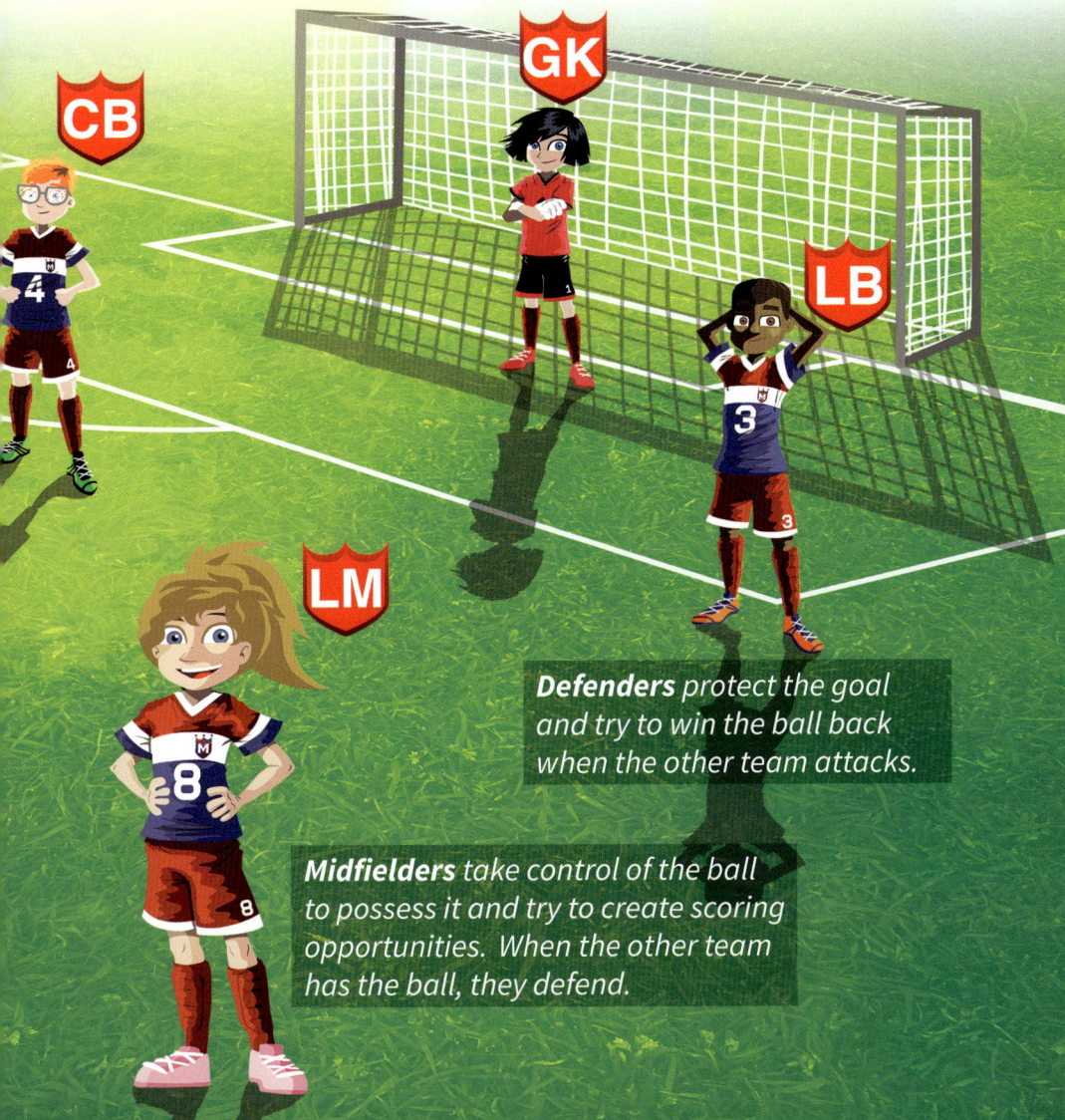

The **goalkeeper** defends the goal and is the only player that can use her hands to handle the ball while it is in the field of play.

GK

CB

LB

LM

Defenders protect the goal and try to win the ball back when the other team attacks.

Midfielders take control of the ball to possess it and try to create scoring opportunities. When the other team has the ball, they defend.

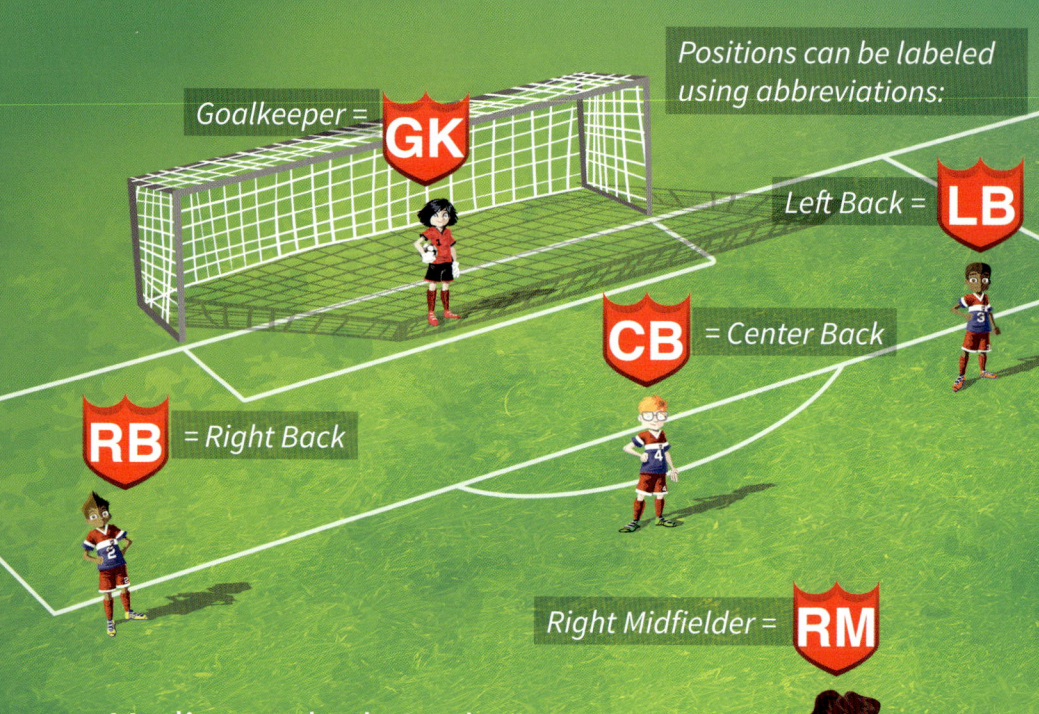

Positions can be labeled using abbreviations:

Goalkeeper = **GK**

Left Back = **LB**

CB = Center Back

RB = Right Back

Right Midfielder = **RM**

Madison asked coach, "Are you sure we're not missing some positions? Aren't there lots of different positions? What about strikers or fullbacks?"

Coach laughed, "Yeah, forwards are sometimes called strikers. Defenders are sometimes called backs. Plus, every position can be right, center or left. There are a lot of options. Your positions will depend on what formation we play."

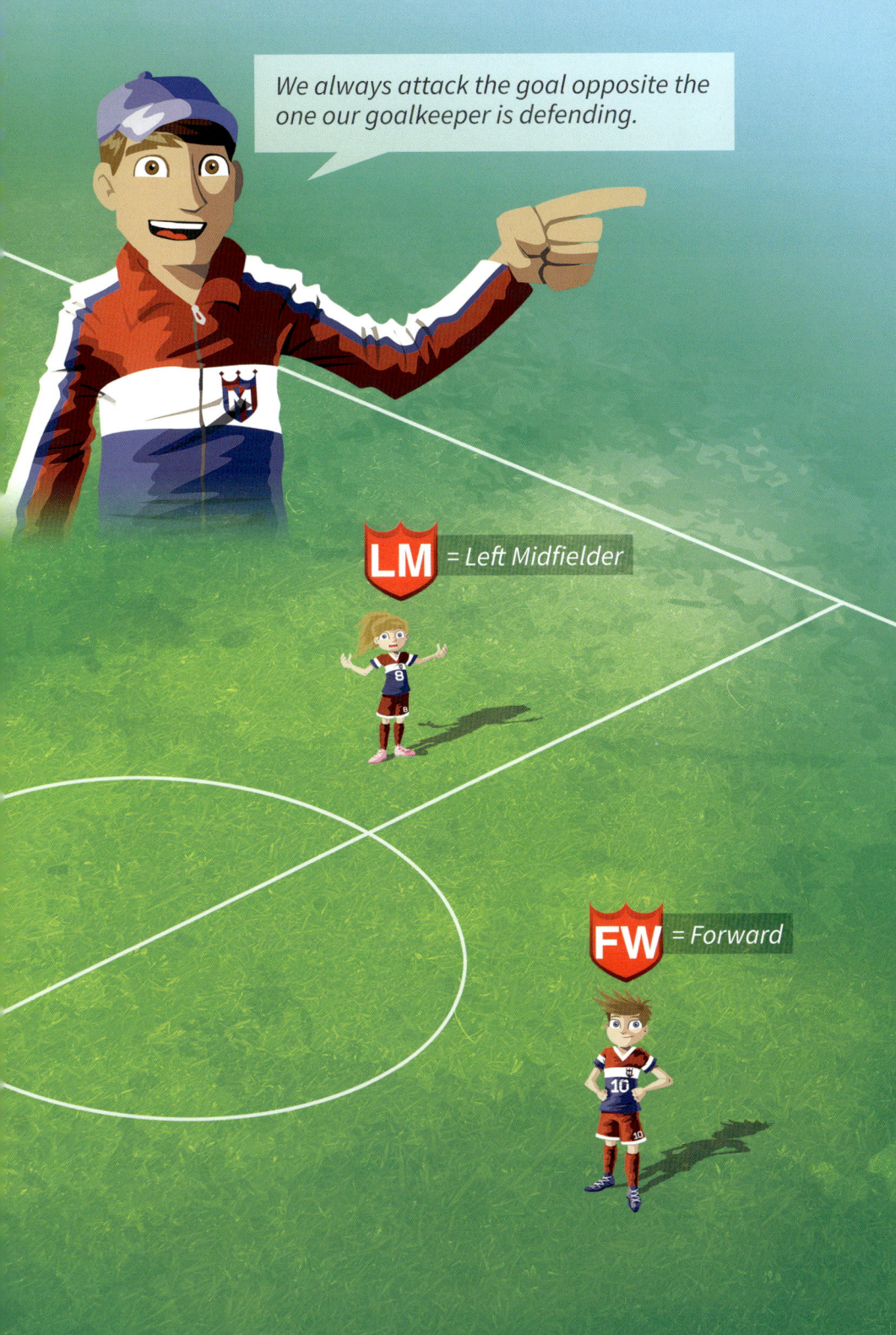

Coach said, "Right now you are in a **formation**. A formation is the shape of all our players on the field. Formations can change based on how many players we use in each position."

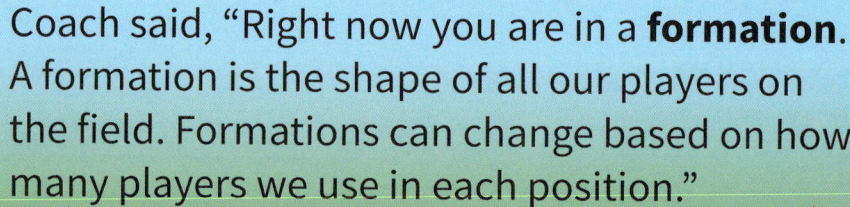

We are in a 3-2-1 formation this week: 3 defenders, 2 midfielders, 1 forward. As you get older and more players are added to each team, we will add more players to each level of position.

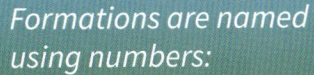

Formations are named using numbers:

There is always a goalkeeper, but they usually don't get a number when formations are discussed.

CB

LB

3-2-1

The first number is the number of defenders.

LM

3-2-1

The second number is the number of midfielders.

FW

3-2-1

The third number is the number of forwards.

I looked at all of my teammates in their positions. We were in rows: the goalkeeper, then the defenders, then the midfielders and then the forwards.

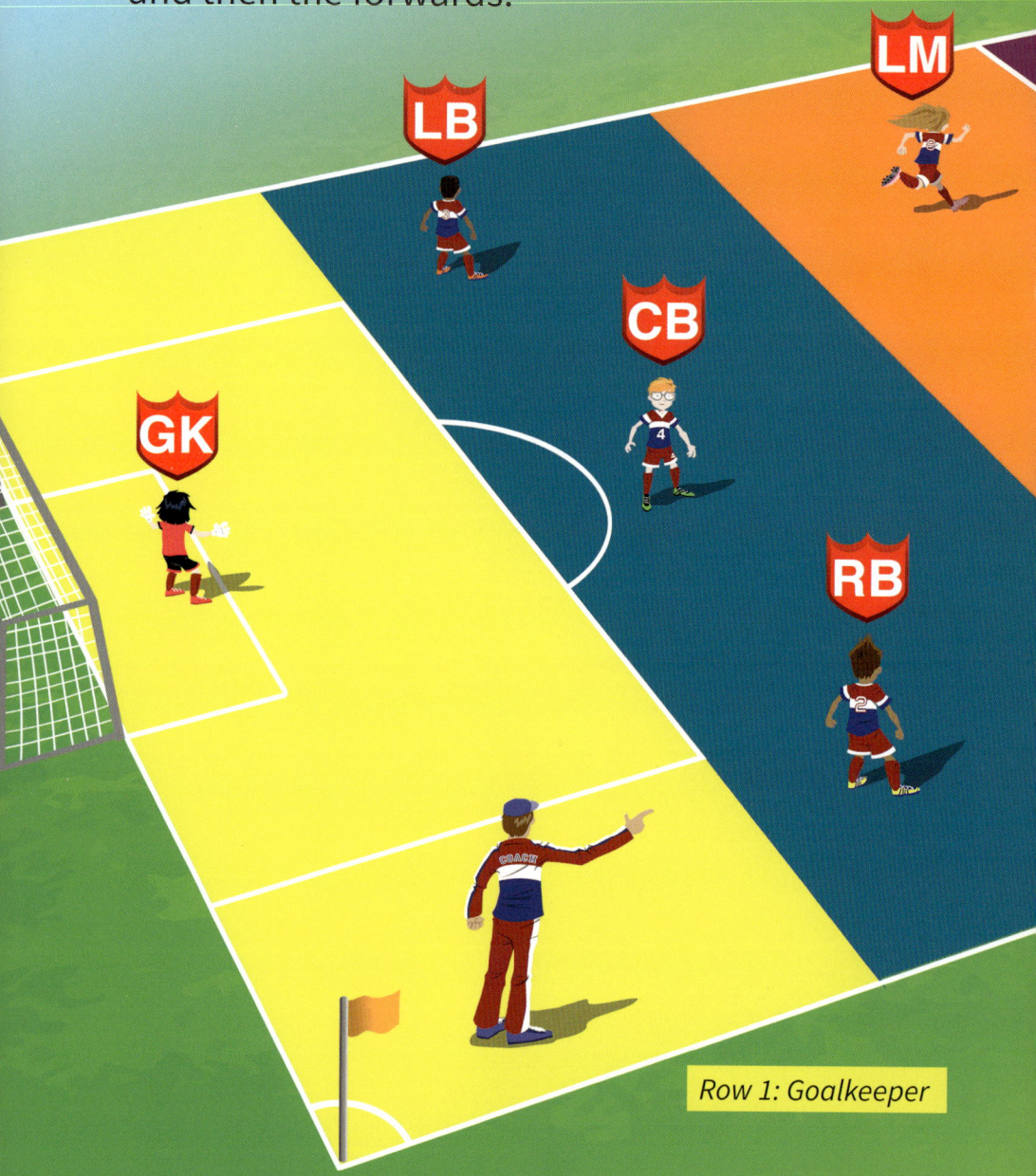

Row 1: Goalkeeper

FW

RM

This season we are playing 7 players against 7. As we get older more players will be added to each row of positions. When we grow up there will be a total of 11 players on each team.

Row 4: Forward

Row 3: Midfielders

Row 2: Defenders

Positions can be thought of as rows on the field.

Coach said, "Your position is not just a space on the field. It is a space between your teammates in the formation. If all of your teammates move forward, you move forward with them. If they move back, you move back. Know where the ball is and keep your **shape** around it."

We spent the next couple of minutes pretending coach was the ball. He moved, and we responded by moving our formation.

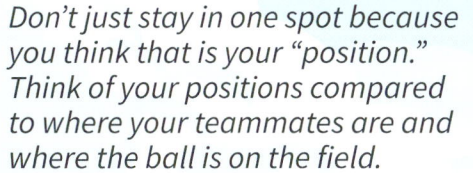

Don't just stay in one spot because you think that is your "position." Think of your positions compared to where your teammates are and where the ball is on the field.

The whole formation has to move to protect the goal and to create scoring opportunities. The formation's shape is kept when the team moves together.

Once we had practiced moving
in formation, Coach threw a ball onto
the field. As soon as the ball hit the grass,
we all ran towards it. Marco got there first.

"Whoa!" Coach said. "Part of being in
formation is spreading out. Don't bunch
up and play pack ball!"

When Marco has the ball his teammates need to be close enough to receive a pass, but they need to be careful not to crowd him.

"When you are spread out, you can pass to each other," Coach said.

Marco was surrounded by other players, so I ran away from him and **showed for the ball**. Bailee cheered! Marco passed the ball to me right away. I laughed and dribbled down the field.

Alex shows for the ball by running between or behind the defenders and letting Marco see him. If Marco chooses not to pass to Alex, Alex needs to move to another space between defenders and show for the ball again.

"Don't be a traffic cone and let the other team just run around you. Move! Remember your position is your space in the formation, not just a spot on the field. Make sure you move to help your teammates attack and defend."

Madison raised her hand again and asked, "How do we stay in position and move with the team and go for the ball? That's a lot to do!"

Even though Marco's place in the formation as left back is usually close to his own goal, when he sees an opportunity to get the ball, he needs to go for it.

"Yes," Coach said, "it is. But you need to do it all. If the ball is close, go for it, but be ready to get back into position."

After he wins the ball and passes to a teammate, Marco needs to quickly return to his position so he and his teammates can keep the team's shape.

And if that wasn't enough, Coach said we also need to cover for each other! "If one of your teammates has to leave their position, someone needs to cover for him," Coach said.

While the right back goes for the ball, his position is empty. His fellow defenders can move closer to cover his position.

After practice, we felt great. We had lots of fun in our positions and realized that no matter who plays what position, we all need to work together as a team to succeed.

Coach said, "Great practice today. You played really hard. It will be confusing for a while. Even the best players in the world still need coaches because they need to learn how to play their positions better every day. You are going to make mistakes, but it doesn't matter how many you make as long as you make them while trying your hardest and playing as fast as you can."

I was still nervous, but I was also really excited. I couldn't wait to play the Dynamo. We were nervous, but we were ready!

Teaching Concepts & Vocabulary

Technique: the ability to efficiently perform a task or specific soccer movement.

Tactic: an action performed by a player or group of players to take advantage of an opponent, group of opponents or a team. The tactics are the tools to develop the strategy.

Strategy: a general plan of action intended to win the game that is agreed upon by the team at the beginning of the game. The strategy relates to the formation and/or system used by the team.

Formation: the shape of the team and distribution of the players on the field at the beginning of the game. This is usually expressed in three numbers identifying the number of players in the defensive, midfield and attacking lines. Example: 4-3-3 indicates 4 defenders, 3 midfielders and 3 forwards.

System: a formation with additional specifications for the shape and/or the roles for one or more players. Systems combine formation and strategy. Example: 4-4-2 with diamond in midfield and outside backs moving up into wide areas.

Keep shape: to stay organized in positions on the field relative to the location of teammates and the ball.

Transition: The switch from playing offense to playing defense, or from defense to offense, which occurs when the ball changes possession. This is often the most important time in any soccer game.

Counter-attack: an immediate attack by one team that is triggered when an attack from the opposing team breaks down and the ball changes possession.

Cover defense: when a teammate is out of position or has been beaten, and the opposing attacking team exploits this area, the defender that is next closest to that area must recognize this and cover the area between his goal and where the attacker has broken through. The next closest player must recognize that event and move to defend the next most dangerous attacker until the attack is slowed and the team can regain its shape.

Pack ball: running with or toward a teammate without purpose and getting in the way of the teammate with the ball, like a puppy that wants to play. It is the failure to open up and create space.

Ball-watching: watching teammates play instead of becoming involved in the action in a positive manner by moving around and helping teammates.

Showing for ball: using movement to present for the ball between or in front of defenders. If the ball isn't passed immediately upon showing for it, the player should move to create a different passing option. Usually the best option is to retreat behind the next closest defender and then move laterally to present for the ball again.

Approach

The iPlaySoccer books Positions 1 & 2 have been specifically designed to assist children in the transition from the 4v4 format of play to the 7v7 format, wherein positioning is formally introduced. The books have attempted to incorporate and apply the principles set forth in US Soccer's 2015 Player Development Initiatives, which were released to the general public in 2015 and requested to be implemented by the calendar year of 2017.

Among those initiatives are recommended positions and formations for both the 7v7 game play format and the 9v9 game play format. Instead of writing separate books for each, we elected to try and simplify these new concepts for children of this age classification by solely utilizing the commonly recommended 3-2-1 formation. We recognize there are many formation options that many very reputable and qualified youth coaches utilize, and by no means do we attempt to dictate what formation a coach elects to use, or attempt to discredit one formation as to another. Rather, these books represent an introduction to the format of play and to some of the concepts and vocabulary players will start to hear at they move along their soccer journey.

Among these new Player Development Initiatives are revised standards which provide for 4v4 play through age 7, and commencing with the U9 age classification the transition to 7v7 play with the introduction of positions, including a goal keeper, the use of formations, and the offside law.

Team Organization

The Team Organization for the U9 and U10 includes a recommendation to utilize either a 2-3-1 formation designed to develop passing and movement of the ball or a 3-2-1 formation designed to promote forward runs and 1v1 situations. US Soccer provided indications as to suggested roles of the players in either position. This assignment of player numbers is remarkable as it represents a suggested style of play.

Traditionally, positions have been assigned a number to correspond with their primary function. The traditional numbering system makes the most sense when viewed within a 4-5-1 formation where the numbering system provides for 4 Defenders, 5 Midfielders, and 1 Forward. While there exist competing numbering systems that may assign different roles to different numbers, a traditional numbering system can be thought of as follows:

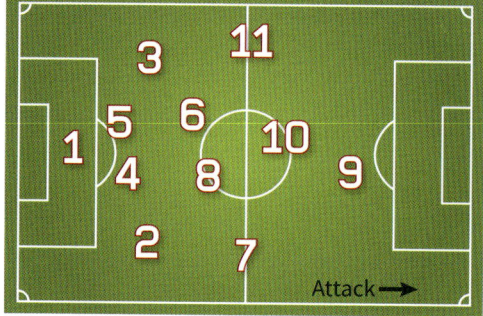

1   **Goalkeeper**: typically a good shot stopper with strong decision making ability and technically proficient in distribution.

2   **Outside Back**: defender with proficiency in 1v1 defending and physically capable to cover the flanks.

3   **Outside back**: plays opposite the Number 2.

4   **Center Back**: defender that is physically strong to win dispositive challenges on the ground and in the air, and must be mentally capable to help organize the defense.

5   **Center Back**: plays opposite the Number 4.

6   **Defensive Midfielder**: defense-oriented player able to cover ground, capable of winning challenges on the ground and in the air and willing to enter into tackles, win and keep possession.

7   **Outside Midfielder/Winger**: must be capable of covering the outside flank, possess a high work rate to make attacking runs but recover to defend, be able to take on defenders 1v1 and provide service into the box.

8   **Center Midfielder**: must be composed and calm on the ball, possess good vision and passing ability, capable of covering a large area of the field and proficient in organizing attacks and defense.

9 **Forward/Striker**: they come in all shapes and sizes, speed and strength are helpful traits along with the ability to win headers as well, but above all, the ability to finish is paramount.

10 **Attacking Center Midfielder**: this playmaking position requires creative, 1v1 attacking, good vision and strong passing ability.

11 **Outside Midfielder/Winger**: plays opposite the Number 7.

Accordingly, in the 3-2-1 formation recommended by US Soccer for 7v7 in the 2015 Player Development Initiatives, they show two Outside Backs as numbers 2 & 3, one Center Back as a number 4, a number 6 Defensive Midfielder and a number 8 Center Midfielder, and one number 9 Forward.

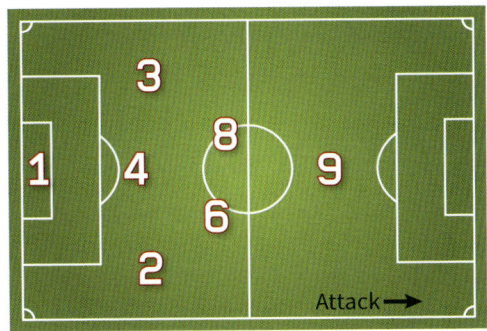

Common Position Abbreviations

G/GK:	Goalkeeper		LM:	Left Midfielder
D/DF:	Defender		RM:	Right Midfielder
RB:	Right Back		CAM:	Central Attacking Midfielder
LB:	Left Back		DM:	Defensive Midfielder
CB:	Center Back		HB:	Half Back (M)
FB:	Full Back (D)		F/FW:	Forward
SW:	Sweeper (D)		CF:	Center Forward
LWB:	Left Wing Back		LF:	Left Forward
RWB:	Right Wing Back		RF:	Right Forward
M/MF:	Midfielder		S/ST:	Striker (F)
CM:	Central Midfielder			

EAT THE RIGHT THINGS!

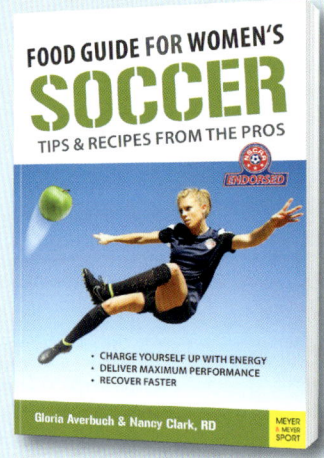

Averbuch/Clark, RD

FOOD GUIDE FOR WOMEN'S SOCCER

TIPS & RECIPES FROM THE PROS

Soccer players are hungry for good nutrition information. This easy-to-read book offers practical tips, debunks nutrition myths, and is a simple "how-to" resource for soccer players, their coaches and parents. Professional soccer players offer advice along with recipes and sample menus.

256 p., in color,
40 photos, 41 illus.,
paperback, 6 ½" x 9 ¼"

ISBN: 9781782550518

$ 18.95 US/$ 32.95 AUS
£ 14.95 UK/€18.95

All information subject to change © Thinkstock/amana images

MOTIVATION AND FUN FOR YOUNG SOCCER PLAYERS

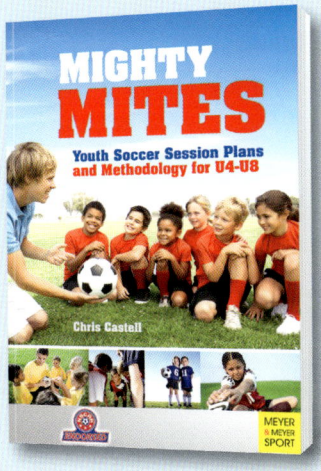

Chris Castell

MIGHTY MITES

YOUTH SOCCER SESSION PLANS AND METHODOLOGY FOR U4-U8

Mighty Mites uses what we know about children and infuses this with soccer. Through stories, we engage young players in soccer. This approach helps coaches accomplish more whilst keeping every player engaged as they all have fun.

136 p., in color,
36 photos, 56 illus.,
paperback, 6 ½" x 9 ¼"

ISBN: 9781782550167

$16.95 US/$29.95 AUS
£12.95 UK/€16.95

MEYER & MEYER Sport
Von-Coels-Str. 390
52080 Aachen
Germany

Phone   +49 02 41 - 9 58 10 - 13
Fax   +49 02 41 - 9 58 10 - 10
E-Mail   sales@m-m-sports.com
Website   www.m-m-sports.com

All books available as E-books.

MEYER
& MEYER
SPORT

Subscribe to our newsletter at **www.m-m-sports.com**

AN INFORMATIVE HANDBOOK
FOR STREET SOCCER COACHES

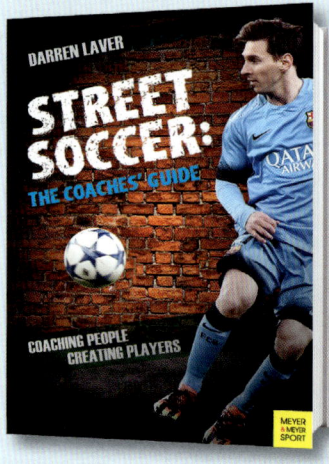

Darren Laver

STREET SOCCER:
THE COACHES' GUIDE

COACHING PEOPLE, CREATING PLAYERS

This guide to street soccer coaching, written by the founder of the International Street Soccer Association (ISSA), is an informative, practical, and easy-to-use handbook for coaches of all levels. It contains 50 games—small sided and 1-v-1—that coaches can try out with their players in order to become more successful and still have fun.

176 p., in color,
c. 100 photos + illus.,
paperback, 6 ½" x 9 ¼"

ISBN: 9781782550518

c. $ 19.95 US/$ 30.95 AUS
£ 13.95 UK/€18.95

All information subject to change © Thinkstock/amana images

MEYER & MEYER Sport
Von-Coels-Str. 390
52080 Aachen
Germany

Phone   +49 02 41 - 9 58 10 - 13
Fax   +49 02 41 - 9 58 10 - 10
E-Mail   sales@m-m-sports.com
Website   www.m-m-sports.com

All books available as E-books.

MEYER
& MEYER
SPORT